© Doug Macomber

CARL PHILLIPS
Rock Harbor

CARL PHILLIPS is the author of six books of poems, including *The Tether* (FSG, 2001), winner of the Kingsley Tufts Poetry Award in 2002, and *From the Devotions*, which was a finalist for the National Book Award. The recipient of an American Academy of Arts and Letters Award in Literature in 2001, he teaches at Washington University in St. Louis.

ALSO BY CARL PHILLIPS

In the Blood

Cortège

From the Devotions

Pastoral

The Tether

Rock Harbor

Rock Harbor

CARL PHILLIPS

FARRAR, STRAUS AND GIROUX

NEW YORK

Farrar, Straus and Giroux
18 West 18th Street, New York 10011

Printed in the United States of America
Published in 2002 by Farrar, Straus and Giroux
First paperback edition, 2003

The Library of Congress has cataloged the hardcover edition as follows:
Phillips, Carl, 1959–
    Rock Harbor / Carl Phillips.— 1st ed.
        p.   cm.
    ISBN 0-374-25140-1 (alk. paper)
    ISBN: 978-0-374-52885-0

    I. Title.

PS3566.H476 R63 2002
811'.54—dc21

                                            2002020588

Paperback ISBN 0-374-52885-3

Designed by Cassandra J. Pappas

www.fsgbooks.com

for Doug Macomber,
for Ellen Bryant Voigt,

and to my parents

Were there then no longing in time, there would be no peace in eternity.

Contents

FIVE

ONE

GOLDEN

There, behind the raised
and extended
wing to which
no bird
no fiend
no haloing is
attached: two bodies,

fucking. It is difficult
to see, but that much—
from the way, with great
then greater
effort, their mouths
seem half to recall or
want to

a song even older,
holier than the one they
fill with—I can
guess. The rest,
I know: that it's dream;
that, in dream,
to know a thing is to

have a gift and
not to, especially. Like
refusing to prove what
anyway all scrutable
signs point to. Stopped
trees are the least of it,
the still standing

but decidedly aslant
version of unanimous,
what looks at
first like approbation;
then—like trees,
and how a wind will
pass through. To turn

with and not
against it
no more means
the wind is with us than
the gods are. I don't
believe each gets what
each deserves.

QUARTER-VIEW, FROM NAUSET

Love, etc. Have been remembering
the part in Sophocles
where a god advises the two heroes

they should be as
twin lions, feeding—how
even the flesh of late

slaughter does not
distract them from keeping
each over the other

a guarding eye.
What part of this is love, and
what survival

is never said,
though the difference it makes is
at least that between a lily and, say,

a shield. I think of you
often, especially here,
at the edge of the world or a

part of it, anyway,
by which I mean of course
more, you will have guessed, than

the coast, just now, I
stand on. Against it,
the water dashes with

the violence of two men who,
having stripped it, now take for their
own the body of

a third man on the bad
sofa of an even worse
motel room in what eventually

is movie—one
we've seen . . . The way
what looks like rape

might not be. You'd like
the light here. At
times, a color you'd call anything but blue.

INTERLUDE

Briefly, an ease

akin to those parts of
the air that

allow the bird respite from
the effort of muscle

flight entails.

As I said: briefly.

It does not matter, I
understand now, my having

hoped in no way to
resemble anyone—

this, the reason
why the difficulty, I have

often been sure, with
death will be less

the dying than the having been
finally always like

everyone else; that
particular

humiliation: to admit
as much.

Very briefly, it
seems now.

In the manner of happiness

or an only-half-grounded
fear or whatever

else can at once
be both pressing and

ignorable, until—as when
the evidence has grown

embarrassing, so why
shouldn't we, let us

throw it away—until it is
like that and, soon, it

is that. We'll assume again

our new positions: myself, at
last arcing

the body
over. —Up. Into yours.

MOVING TARGET

If to be patient were less
an exercise

and more a name to be worn, say,
in the middle—

that he might wear it—

Of the linen sash to
his robe, of linen,

that his hands have
fashioned a knot such that
the knot suggests now a dragonfly in

flight from what is harmless and

not, entirely—
that he might, if at all, know this

only as when without understanding it
we know we have and have come to

expect we shall have always

upon others
an effect we do not
intend—

His face:

a face, turning. And
then a turned one.

CORRAL

for Percival Everett

Fleetingly, the mule is neither
justice nor injustice, but
another muscled

abbreviation in which
right and wrong take in
each other no apparent

interest, as if—impossible, on
purpose—to remind how
not everything is

vengeance, not everything
wants reason. The mule
intends nothing of the contrast he

makes inevitably
in a field otherwise all
horses: five of them, four

standing around and nosing
the only one whose flesh, white
entirely, lacks pattern, unless

the light counts,
the only one not standing,
lying with the particular

stillness of between when
a death has occurred
already and when we

ourselves shall have
learned of it. Until then,
that which before was

patternless and not standing
stands up, white, patterned
by the countable light,

the five horses step
into then just past a shy
gallop, the mule

among them, then beside them,
the mule falling in time behind
slightly, not like defeat—don't

think it—like instead one who,
understanding (as a mule
cannot) in full the gravity

of the truth always that he carries
with him, can
afford to pity

honestly a glamour that
extends even to the legs, classical,
on which each horse for now outruns the mule.

AS A BLOW, FROM THE WEST

Names for the moon:
Harvest; and Blue; and
Don't Touch Me—

and Do. I dreamed I had
made a home on the side
of a vast, live volcano,

that the rest was water,
that I was one among many of
no distinction: we but

lived there, like so many
birds that, given the chance
not to fly for once in

formation, won't take it, or
cannot, or—or—but
what of choice can a bird know?

Down the volcano's sides,
in the pose of avalanche
except frozen, and so

densely it seemed impossible
they should not strangle
one another—yet they

did not—grew all
the flowers whose names
I'd meant to master;

it was swift, the dream—so
much, still, to catch
up to—though I could not

have known that, of course,
then: isn't it only in
the bracing and first wake of

loss that we guess most cleanly
the speed with which what held us
left us? In the dream, the world

was birdless, lit, yielding, it
seemed safe, which is not to say
you weren't in it. You were, but

changed somewhat, not so much
a man of few words,
more the look of one who

—having entered willfully
some danger, having just returned
from it—chooses instead

of words his body as
the canvas across which to
wordlessly broadcast his coming

through. We lived
in a manner that—if it
didn't suggest an obliviousness

to a very real and always-there
danger—I would call heady;
it was not that. Think,

rather, of the gods: how,
if they do in fact know
everything, they must understand

also they will be eventually
overthrown by a new order,
which is at worst a loss

of power, but not of life,
as the gods know it. I was
not, that is, without

ambition: the illicit, in
particular, I would make it
my business to have studied;

and of that which is gained
easily, to want none
of it. Flowers; names

for the moon. It was
swift, the dream, the body
a wordless and stalled

avalanche that, since forgivable—
if I could—I would forgive, poor
live but flagging, dying now

volcano. And the water
around its sides receding with
a dream's swiftness: everywhere,

soon, sand and sand, a desert that,
because there was no water,
and because they missed it,

the natives had called a sea, and
to the sea had given a name:
Friendship, whose literal

translation in the country of
dream is roughly "that which
all love evolves

down to"—

Until to leave, or
try to—and have drowned

trying—becomes refrain,
the one answer each time
to whatever question:

what was the place called?

what was the house like?

what was it we did inside it?

how is it possible that it cannot be enough to have given
up to you now the dream as—for a time, remember—I did
     give

my truest self? why won't you take it—if a gift, if yours?

THE CLEARING

Had the light
changed, possibly—or,

differently, was that how I'd
seen it

      always, and not
looking? Was I meant for

a vessel? Did I only
believe so and,

so, for a time, was it true but

only in that space which belief makes
for its own wanting?

What am I going to
do with you
          —Who just

said that?

Whose the body—where—that voice
belongs to?

                    Might I turn,
toward it, whinny

into it?

            My life
            a water,

            or a cure for
            that which no water
            can cure?

            His chest
            a forest, or a lush
            failure—

Even now, shall I choose? Do I
get to?

Dearest-once-to-me

                    Dearest-still-to-me

Have I chosen
already,

        or is choice a thing
hovering yet, an

intention therefore, from
which, though
late, could I hurry back?

What am I going to do with you— or

how?
Whom for?

            If stay my hand—where

    rest it?

THE DEPOSITION

Whether it more was like
the ocean,
or more

those plates in the earth that
shift abruptly according to
laws that, even if I

give to them here
no name, apply
nevertheless outside, in

spite of—
I forget,
as so many somewhere always have

just said. Exaggeration,
to say I never thought
I'd lie among them; more exactly: I

had not hoped to. How
brief, comparatively
at least, that

feathered phase—
less Roman,
more Greek, more

birch than
ash, none of shame's
nobility attached, but—

worse—the embarrassing
thud of blunder, to
ever have laid

the blue-to-black,
black,
then blue

familiar of self full-length
and down, ringside, as if there'd been
a ring, or as if by

long traveling at last done
in, as who would
not be? I

had not guessed it.
As when to find a stone
is to find revealed

no truth unless the truth
of stones, which
is to say the fact of

themselves only. Or
as when the song
of wanting is understood as

not at all the song of
being wanted,
not like thirst,

not like hunger,
not the disappointment
of only the one leaf gone

vermilion inside of
the tree's saffron majority,
not a godlessness in

the wake of a habit of prayer, neither
that sort of wind, nor a tunnel, or through one, it
was not like that.

TWO

BY HARD STAGES

All the glories—
ribbed, and
separate,

      collective
sway-in-the-wind.
Shut them.

      To have wanted
more, where has that
carried me,

      if what
so much matters
now can be proven

later to all
along have been doomed
not to?

    ◆

      The governing
drift was from
sensation to

distraction to
irrelevance: "they came
to nothing," it says here,

"en route
settling for things like
heat falling mostly

against, light mainly
falling, between them
a bush or

a skull
shimmering like another
example of absence of

will—with
heat only,
shivering—"

◆

Do I make
a difference? or
What is it

       so persuades, I
must make one?
The text breaks like a road

forking where none
warned of . . .
Look at yourself,

Look at you.
       Have I not
looked there—

possibility for
—into it?
       How small,

    ◆

without effort almost,
can be the leap from
it-is-findable to

we-have-found-it.
Though not water,
not the flash, even,

as if off of that which
could be water, could
also not be—

            To have
called it water. "They
crossed themselves,

they gave
utterly themselves over
to what

          wasn't there,
that it might
save, or drown them . . ."

THE CLARITY

No dream—but as

if so, moving at first
with the force of

idea purely; and
then of a man convinced
he has justified

brilliantly himself to
himself; and then
of the yearling that,

haltered at
last, remains
still to be gentled, to be

broken-to-ride, although
no yearling, not a horse
ever, and not dream.

I turned.
I could see,
across the room,

heaped there like fouled
linen like memory like
detritus stepped

away from, the truth of
—of myself: glintless,
yes, but no

more so for my having (how
long?) disavowed it.
Suggestive of sorrow,

or the cool irreversibility that
attaches commonly to
larger mistakes

of judgment—so did it
lie there: undiminished.

I take it, in the darkness, to my face.

LOOSE HINGE

Of the body: most,
its resilience, have you
not loved that, its—its

endingness,
that too?
And the unwitting

prayer getting made
between them,
as when we beat at

what is closed,
closed against us, and call
the beating, in time,

song. To have been
among the hands
for which the stone lets go

its sword,
or the tree its gold
crepitating

bough,
what must that
feel like? With what speed

does the hero grow
used to—necessarily—
the world's surrender

until—how
else—how call it
strange, how

not inevitable? Heroes,
in this way at least, resembling
the damned

who are damned
as traitors, some
singing *We could not*

help it, others
Fate,
Circumstance,

X
made me—as if
betrayal required more than

one party, which it
does not.
Admit it: you gave

yourself away. We are
exactly what
we are, as you

suspected, and—
like that—the world
obliging with its fair

examples: rain and,
under it, the yard
an overnight field

of mushrooms,
the wet of them, the yellow-
white of, the

nothing-at-all, outside
themselves, they
stood for. You've been

a seeming
exception only. Hot;
relentless. Yourself the rule.

THE THRESHING

A sweetness, say—
and coming, on me. Or, in
almost-squares,

light dismissible at
first as that which,
surely— Did I

dream that?
Between
what by now lies far

behind, and what
ahead still, gets
forged a life that,

whether or not I can
recall having
called it mine own

—or say so
now—will have been
the case, notwithstanding:

as when a smaller
fate, this time, fumbles
clear of one larger, flies

free, how the usual
questions—is this
nature? design?

whose?—
alter none of the
particulars of escape,

of the being foiled.
If the world is
godless, then

an absence I am
always with, and
it with me. Or

else the world is
stitched with gods and
unavoidably I am

with them,
they with me.
To be reduced to

nothing, literally, but a life
to lose; to surrender
that, also, to those

whispering *Yes, yes,*
that also— Isn't this
the idea? To give, even

full well knowing that
they might take it,
they might not, their

gaze—as if by some
city more new
and glittering than

the last one graced
briefly then lifted
out of—their gaze

distracted.
Point at which
who seeks, with the

swerveless patience that
hunger, for a time,
affords, shall find

his target—stilling,
stopped. No room
for wanting. —Was this

not the idea?
The hands: as if only
made for this—

Should the eyes not
be, already,
shut,

then you must shut them.

THE SILVER AGE

Naturally, the lawn fills
in, where you
repaired it.

Of the two
trees left,

one dying,

the parts of the tree
across which disease gets
laid, like a map,
out,

and the other parts,
putting forth still their
late, bright,
October buds—berries—

which one?

What's to
stay for, in a slow
drama whose end we know
already?

                This morning,
it seems impossible,

that question, to have ever
asked it,

that I did not
always recognize
a pleasure—

baroque,
acquired—findable
only inside the particular

chord that an ever-building body
of evidence

makes, finally,
with the very fact it can't
help but

lead to.

                After which, though
a bit surprised where,
before, was hope, or

doubt, *We suspected
as much*, we say. *We knew*

all along

what the light would
be like—
a grazing

weightlessness; what

leaves, in turn;

sprawl of the sleeper's
legs

his chest

his face

TO BREAK, TO RIDE

That, nightly,
some blooms fold,
some open; how

the opossum at the same
hour forages the same swatch
of yard; and the moth,

a shadow, all
over again navigates
more shadow—

There's a knowing born
of conquering;
conscious at first,

or never, reflexive finally,
a mastery of pattern,
how a thing changes—

light,
a difference in it,
an absence of—

the better to mark and
react in turn to
when, of a sudden, pattern

stops: where
is danger?
what is safe? This

kind of knowing, it is like
a ladder. It is
scales, in music:

though I believe that the earth
rotates, what I
notice more is

the moon appearing,
what I'd rather
remember is another

story—concerns a boat,
routine, the bearing
away of one

brightness, the fact
of others,
smaller, more of. How

still, beside me. The difference
between us the same as
that between a garden

shaped by patience,
attention,
plan,

and a field to which
an unexpected heat in late
October brings

now the worker bees
confused, instinctive,
back. If a sadness

to it, then
a sadness, one that
no more lets me go than

I let *it* go. It is waste,
to worry. We shall never
be more close than we are now.

ENTRY

As if an ark—
or,

like one, how slow . . .

How it does not seem
to leave the shore or
want to so much as—more,

whatever it must, already, it is
letting go.

On the water, a stillness that
should not be
so terrible. Why

is it? What so satisfied,
before, about distortion

that, now, I miss it?

There should be birds,

sky-strung, and

following, isn't that what
happens in the wake,
at first, of a sea

departure? To have
ever heard such or—once

heard—to have
trusted in it—

Which is worse,
the incidental, or the more
deliberate? How

much of what seems
deliberate isn't, is

instead unavoidably

inherent, a fact
of character, of the self
no one chooses—

incidental, therefore. The blame
that lies always

somewhere matters
here—seems to—no
more than whether I wave or don't

at the nothing, almost, left
to wave at. I am

farther, even, than I imagined,

or hoped for, or

against— Which?

There should be custom,
conduct, some

compass fashioned out of
rules by which to fix
not on failure's

occurrence—what needs

no marker—but on,
of that occurrence, what degree

exactly. Surely even a
precision concerning

the difficult-to-admit-to will have
had its pleasures? The air,
for example, heavy,

less with blooming than with

the thought of. A collapse

of vision; the rise,
accordingly, of craft—

here,
between the two, where neither
one, to the other, gives

ever itself up

entirely, the narrowest space,
opening:
it shuts behind me.

THREE

BLUE SHOULDER

Come here.
See how the boughs pass
idly over, across

one another, return
after, as a hand
can do

with what never will be
possessed—only
wanted, touched only—

and then to its original position come
less unpunished than
untempted toward what is punishable

back slowly.
                    This is the way
a house shakes

in a wind—the way, in the throat,
song does. Hear it? This is
the kind of rain that

so much looks like not
stopping, we get used to it,
an end to falling becomes

the last thing we expected,
and—there, an ending. I think
pleasure is like that, or

can be, I think
you are.
          The snow,

what remains of it, slides
melted, free from an earlier
stranding-place among

storm-stunted rhododendrons—
the leaves in turn find
again the pose of here-no-there

remembering,
or asking,
what did a snowlessness

once resemble? To ask as much
maybe should not
be to open, however

narrow, a door
on suffering—I think it can be. If you
will not stay, go now.

SPOKEN PART,
FOR COUNTERTENOR VOICE

I. Carolina Window

Through the glass, spillage—

no longer half-explaining
the story—becomes the story:

limb   tree   thicket
until, further, the wooded miles.

A field of view, which is to say
finite. Making what is
continuous and whole

seem discrete, divisible, as
if to the material world and our
vision of it could be assigned
the same properties, which

is impossible—a variety, at
best, of hoping. Not hope itself.

II. Window, Graham Chapel

Against the figured pane
the hours lean, almost—

time a ghost, granted only
part of its wish: substance, but
without visibility. —Color, or
the light, angling shine,

something gives to the face
of Christ the look of one who
understands, like never before,

damage as the song with which
the sleeve of God comes lined.

Necessity to shadow, as any
wind to the branch inside it.

There's a flaw in the glass.

ROCK HARBOR

The wind was high—it gave to your
hair a lift in equal parts gradual,
steep, disarming—

                I love a storm,
and said so; by *I have always*
loved better the wreckage after,

I did not mean instead of, but
a preference.
              To the air, an edge

anyone would call arctic—isn't
that why we left it nameless? To
your face, a look I'd admired before

in the bodies of those who seem
not so much indifferent as made
ignorant, or stunned as if by

sudden luck, or else repentant and
in payment, somehow, for what
all price falls like an irrelevance,

a stole, an expensive sail in a
calm away from. Sex
as a space available where neither

loss nor regret figures—imagine
that.
        Or not having, finally, to take

anything away—in the form of
photographs of the mostly ice
that the harbor's water, the shore

past that, the street after had
become; or as words like those
that came to me: *green, kind of,*

lit almost, but as if from within
in places, a spill but
an arrested one, less force than

the idea of it, block and edge like
the chance for pattern, but
spent now or only, from the very

start, false
                —false and singing.
The wind was high; it exaggerated

what you were already, a man
returning toward shelter he can't
see yet, but believes just ahead

exists, the sort of man for whom
to doubt at all is treason. By
not unfaithful, I understood I

could mean both things: I'd do
nothing I'd promised not to—
Also, there is nothing I'll forget.

FOUR

TRADE

Bending—as no
flower bends—
casting the difficult rule

of his attention upon an elsewhere
that accordingly broke open
into a splendor that, too,

would pass,
I am resigned,
mostly,

said the emperor,
to a history between us less of loss than,
more protractedly, of losing—

and, having said as much, said
nothing else to the man to
whom he'd said it;

whom, for years now, he'd called
variously paramour,
consort,

sir; who, for
himself, said nothing;
who from where he was seated could

see, and easily,
each at its labeled and color-coded slip
moored slackly,

the bows of the ships of the Fleet
Imperial, about which
what he found, just

then, most worth admiring it
is impossible, anymore, to
say exactly:

the trim of them,
flawless, sleek—reminiscent, in
that way, of almost any line from Ovid; or

when there was wind,
how the bows tipped,
idly,

in it;
or the stillness, afterwards,
that they found; or the way they seemed to.

TO THE TUNE OF A SMALL, REPEATABLE, AND PASSING KINDNESS

In the cove of hours-like-a-dream this
is, it isn't so much
that we don't enjoy watching

a view alter rather little, and each time
in the same shift-of-a-cloud
fashion. It's the

swiftness with which we
find it easier, as our cast
lines catch more and more at nothing,

to lose heart—
                        All afternoon, it's
been with the fish as with

lovers we'd come to think of as
mostly forgotten, how
anymore they less often themselves

surface than sometimes
will the thought of them—less
often, even, than that, their names . . .

But now the fish bring to mind
—of those lovers—
the ones in particular

who were knowable
only in the way a letter written
in code that resists

being broken fully can be
properly called a letter we
understand: *If*

you   a minute   could you   when
said I might   however
what if   haven't I loved

—who?
            As I remember it, I'd lie
in general alone, after, neither in

want nor—at first—sorry inside
the almost-dark I'd
wake to. The only stirring

the one of last light getting
scattered, as if for
my consideration. All over the room.

CAVALRY

The best views—the ones
from horseback—will be
no longer: surely no one can

fail to see how
the horses, perishing, are
all but done for. Already, though,

the idea of infantry
rears before us—a prospect
we find not without its

portion, more than fair, of
invitation. So much
as well, meanwhile, will go

unchanged: the peculiar,
undistracted
sorrow attached to

bugle call, at sunset, a sorrow
finally that of inquiry
itself, whose modes are two:

to branch,
to cluster,
manifesting itself in

panicles, as of lilacs, the still
remembered stoop we called
bluebells, if blue—if white,

snowdrops, wasn't
that it,
when we knew no better than

to name the light at dusk
flirtation,
for how it seemed

each night like—
first—going,
then gone forever, and then

came back. It seems less to have
been flirtation—more,
a career spent saying,

perpetually,
farewell, until
who believes it? Even now,

we have only to lift
long enough our
faces, the light

again gives what it
always has to flesh,
a color that makes

briefly forgettable how
the art of casting bronze
is a mostly

lost one.
There seems nothing that is
impossible. Soon, darkness;

we'll put the horses down,
a mercy. We'll salvage, find
rest beside their still

good-for-trade
saddles: cool, and
wet, by morning.

TO SPEAK OF IT NOW

Leaving, he conducted his
body as if it were that of a child
Pharaoh, who

understands to a sometimes
dimming,

brightening other times,

degree the possibilities for
great power,

has been told it somewhere
rests finally inside
himself.

How he will use it,

whether he will or won't
live to do so, neither
the hand, ring-heavy, nor

the head beneath its abbreviated
tower of crown

quite answers.

North of here, in a country he
won't ever know of,

snow falls like the part
of argument where
all room for argument now

diminishes,
is gone, becomes like
dream that

—did it happen?
Made small

by distance,

through a window,

the people he does not easily yet
call his own
seem the pinchings-off

of clay,
what gets forgiven that it is dirty

by the ease with which it can be
shaped into something beautiful that
also serves.

That *he* thinks of them, though,
that way, is
less than believable, it is

unlikely still he considers them much
at all.

He is quiet mostly. This

does not mean that if asked to
name, among the world's most

lovely things,

the second—or if third,
a close one—he

would not know.

The Nile by moonlight.

The Nile with the stars upon it.

THOSE PARTS THAT RESCUE LOOKED LIKE

The usual, pulled, expansive
afternoon—the flattish
light of it less

disclosure, more a stripping from
the field its
small details—

I had almost forgotten that definition
requires shadow. I had
been distracted, had found

myself among the ones who would be
persuaded, singing as if
of song were made the ship called Self-

Persuasion: *we shall not*
want what we do not
miss, we cannot

miss what we don't
remember . . .
                    But if persuasion is

not a ship? if
no persuasion? —I
did not ask. I'd forgotten, almost,

that to want to know a life
entirely is not
the worst thing: obliteration,

for example, is worse—
one familiarity, by another,
getting canceled; or,

inside one, getting
lost, which is
worse still, oblivion,

less to escape from than to
lie not-touching-not-touched-by
beside an agony that

is, to love, as
shadow is to light—as,
to the body, is penetration.

I had forgotten: almost
all of it, the time of year, of
light making of—for hours—the field

a flatness, even
song itself, I
shall not want, I cannot

miss, the notes not
notes any longer but
something ravenous and—in their

flight, as from
parts of sky more
turbulent

toward others, clearer—marking
without marking the crossed, crossed
again field

beneath them, less their shadows,
more what shadow gave, more
everything it darkened.

VIA SACRA

The horse rides easy.
Intermittently,
that I can ride at all, still, can

seem the miracle that everyone
here calls it; that I ride
well—

what words?
Roadside,
the marigolds look for

all the world that
yet is knowable as
if they knew, impossibly, that

in a country not far, not
this one, their
petals are considered worth

gathering first in
shallow bowls, then
whispering a prayer over and just

past.
That I might never be estranged (from
what, though?), might be

instead what is meant, precisely, when
some sing
     Spotless;

     Immaculate
          —others, singing.
The candles they carry

are of beeswax,
from a believing, once, that bees
were virgin-born. They aren't, but

by that logic, unbleached
let be the linen the veil is made of, whether
purple, violet,

blue—draped across, of every house,
its eastern wall, to show divinity
has hid itself, has

 left. It is as if the world were
boat, and God its keel; or the world
is bird—God its breastbone, ourselves

the left-to-our-own-devices
acolytes defining with rods
of willow a boundary we cross

and cross,
a story, a blind man in the crowd and
stepping free. He takes to his eyes

the longing with which our course,
behind, lies strewn, he
is unblinded. First thing he sees: a boy

who stammers; who's
let his candle fall.

THE USE OF FORCE

Framed by window, the branches
swim in place, they
seem to. No

wonder struggling gets
so often, at first, mistaken
for wild abandon: a very

likeness.
Difference matters,
as in: in you, a permanence

you have known, that
I shall never. As in:
the two of us regarding

equally but differently
the sea,
the sea, in

equal but different parts.
Distinction matters. Distraction
loves us. Attention

must be paid, else we are
happier, yes, but what we were
lies ended— Did I really

think that, ever?
Do I?
A history of forgetting

is not the same as
a habit of it, though
history is not

unconcerned with pattern,
and pattern is to habit
as a kind of twin whose hair,

parted leftside instead of right,
prevents an otherwise
confusion. As between, say,

the man who in crime finds
a taste he gradually, slow, more
and more comes

into; and the man who, like
any criminal
worth admiring, admires

precision, the angle beyond which
the victim's neck, bent
back, perforce

must break. *Hold still*, you said. I
did.
The proof is vision.

FIVE

RETURN TO THE LAND OF THE
GOLDEN APPLES

Blue wash. The winged horses look
like horses—artless, free
of connotation. They hide

just now their wings,
or they forget, or do not
think to make

much more of a gift
for flight than
of the water viewable

behind them—a sea,
a lake—
which they ignore, pulling

at the record-of-where-a-wind-was,
the now-resist-now-don't,
and other flowers

whose growth has even
outstripped the grass, the colors
wind as far as the ruined tower, up

even to the room that
crowns it, over the half moss, half
ledge of window, glassless,

into the room, which is small,
not empty: the body,
and a mirror. Inside

the mirror, the body
turning, stopping,
—sometimes the way, in

sudden shadow, will any
animal; sometimes,
as the hero stops

in the gathering light of reputation
he soon must recognize
is his own. The body

inside the mirror, turning,
singing *I am the one who forces,*
I am the one who stays

to watch,
I am the grit gone somehow
shine, the blow,

the forced thing, opening
—Singing inside the mirror,
to no one, to

itself, the body folding, and
unfolding—as if
map, then shroud—its song.

FLIGHT

If blackness
were every blankness, and not
all colors, if

wings were parts to be lifted
easily from the body, then brought
back home, and the wings

tipped first in yellow,
in red, after,
would any of these make the bird

more yours?
If the bird is native here,
and you are native,

so that seeing it now is not
a first time, seeing,
what happened then, that since

has acted upon memory
as on photographs
will a creek they've fallen into,

the water bleeding, making
ghost of now the tree somebody
climbs halfway,

the parked car others take
forever boarding, and the field raveling,
prairie, then sea . . .

What would be different, wouldn't
each change equal ruin the way
it does, and the hands that clap

still be your own,
clapping? To watch the bird
undone, undoing—isn't *that* it?

FRETWORK

      Reports are various—
conflicting also:

many fell,
      a few;

like taken cities . . .

    ◆

Whether or not
to any loss there is weight
assignable,

       or a music given

—some play of notes,
slow-trumpeted,

for which to listen
is already to be
too late;

      whether forgetting is
or is not proof of
mercy, henceforth let

others say.

◆

     Is not victory itself
the proof of victory?

◆

Little hammer, chasing—onto
unmarked metal—pattern,
decoration,

a name,

a scar upon the face
of history, what

has no face

◆

     Of briar
and thorn, my bed.

◆

—I stand in clover.

RAVAGE

He has made me to know,
in myself, a compassion I have
no use for.

He fairly breaks—as they say—my heart.

He passes into and free of the light,

the light itself
trophaic in its semblance
of taking leave.

Clouds;
late fog:

he has caused me to understand
and record
the difference,

as between the sea when
it seems mostly a delicate, black

negotiation

and the sky at night when it wants
for stars.

Wild bird

at rest
in the very hand to which it once was blur
entirely,

all resistance—

Had I not
called it a thing done with
already, the better part

of pleasure? Did he not find me

lying still
in the part at least I had thought

to keep?

CANOE

The brow of a man who,
when he takes to his own
another's body, means

somewhere also *I would
like to help*.
          The lake a compass,

the canoe its needle,
ourselves inside
that—

      The way
what's missing can go
unnoticed beside what's there,

until we notice: these
were his arms,
now raised, now dropped,

lifting.
      Slight pockings,
like the chips that give

historically more character
to marble retrieved
after long burial,

bust of
the emperor Hadrian
in that period just

past the death, on purpose,
of his boy favorite.
                  Lilies,

lilies.
        Watch, he said; and
bringing the paddle

up, vertical, leaving
only the blade submerged
—stilling the blade—

he dragged the water:
we were turning . . .
                  Lost,

as a thing
can be, beyond all calling
of it back—none, anymore,

calling—
        It seemed related to
what I'd heard

about cars, ice,
steer always
into the skid's direction—

those lessons where
to have learned means nothing
next to having had

to apply.
I want forgiveness to be as easy as the gestures for it, it
isn't, is it?

JUSTICE

Nameless, or else
many-named, no matter,
but the dog must come

with an allegiance heightened,
almost, to machine.
I want her lean,

I want her hungry. I want her
ruthless, or not at all.
Mornings,

let her lick the grass dry
of dew, my tired hands,
by night, of the lives

unwittingly, indifferently,
they've touched. Oh,
who is heartless?

Ghost-dog. Mirror-dog.
Shadow whose every move is
nothing, nothing without

what casts it.
Let even the most
trained of eyes

find the difference
between us
hard measuring. Of

that which cannot be
had entirely, understand:
I'll have no part. No

feathers, then—blue,
obvious; nor the yellow
undershaftings, either,

that the otherwise mostly
spatter-and-bronze
flicker shows best

in flight.
No.
Let the dog be

ever memorial to that
precision that makes geometry
more than seem, again,

worth trusting: the gun
—raised, fired—the line
traceable from where hit to

where the bird, broken, falls,
and the dog knowing, already,
where—making

for it . . . *Bring it back.*
Give. Only then. Let her
drop the bird whole—dead,

undamaged,
mercy—
from her mouth. And want no more.

MINOTAUR

What stalked the room was never envy.
Is not regret, anymore,

nor fail. We are
—discovered:

we resemble hardly
ever those birds now, noising but
not showing from their double
cloisters—
leaves,
fog.

I miss them.

I forget what I wanted to
mean to you.
                I forget what I
meant to give to you, that I haven't.

Ménage.
You, in sleep still,
the dog restless, wanting

out, like a dream of the body caught
shining inside a struggling whose
end it cannot know will be
no good one.

Outside, the basil shoots to flower; the neighbors'
burro, loose, astray, has
found the flowers, his

head enters and tilts
up from the angle confusable with
sorrow,
adoration. His hooves pass

—like God doing, for now,
no damage to them—

the heirloom tomatoes: Beam's Yellow Pear,
Russian Black,
Golden Sunray, what sweetness once
looked like, how it tasted
commonly.

All that time.

I have held faces lovelier—lovelier, or
as fair.
      They make sense
eventually. Your own begins to:

fervor of a man
cornered; unuseful tenderness with which,

to the wound it won't survive, the animal
puts its tongue.

HALO

In the dream, as if to remind
himself of his own power—that he
does have some—the gelding

whinnies once,
once more, at
nothing passing.

If this were song, I'd call it *Someone*
Waving from Across the Water
at Someone Else

Not Waving Back,
but it is dream. You, speaking; and I
distracted as usual

from the words, this time by
how you speak them;
the way tuberoses open,

or new leafage—
slow, instinctive; sexual
vaguely.

There is little I've not done for you.
There are questions.
There are answers I do not give.

Between the sometimes terrible
(because leaving us always) fact
of the body to which we're

each, each moment, eroded
down—between our bodies
and the pattern the light,

dreamlight, is making on them,
the effect is one of trade routes
long since confused by time, war,

a forgetfulness, or
because here, and here, as from
much handling, the map

especially has gone soft:
wind as a face gone red with blowing,
oceans whose end is broken stitchery—

swim of sea-dragon, dolphin,
shimmer-and-coil, invitation . . . You know
the kind of map I mean. Countries as

distant as they are believable,
than which—to find,
to cross—I am not

more difficult. *Here I am*, I say,
wanting to help,
Over here. And you turn. And

on its axis—swift,
inexorable as luck—the dream, turning,
with you . . .

Acknowledgments

Grateful acknowledgment is made to the following publications, in which the poems in this volume first appeared:

Boston Review: "The Deposition"

Callaloo: "Golden," "Quarter-view, from Nauset," "Interlude," "Moving Target," "The Clearing"

Daedalus: "The Use of Force"

Field: "Canoe"

Green Mountains Review: "Entry," "Those Parts That Rescue Looked Like"

The Harvard Advocate: "To Speak of It Now"

Indiana Review: "The Silver Age," "Minotaur"

The Kenyon Review: "As a Blow, from the West"

Kestrel: "Loose Hinge"

LIT: "Blue Shoulder," "Cavalry"

Michigan Quarterly Review: "Rock Harbor," "Return to the Land of the Golden Apples"

Mid-American Review: "The Threshing," "To the Tune of a Small, Repeatable, and Passing Kindness"

New England Review: "The Clarity," "Justice"

The New Republic: "Flight"

Parnassus: Poetry in Review: "To Break, to Ride," "Trade," "Via Sacra"

The Progressive: "Corral"

Seneca Review: "Ravage," "Halo"

The Threepenny Review: "Fretwork"

Tikkun: "By Hard Stages"

"The Clearing" also appeared in *The Best American Poetry 2001* (Robert Hass and David Lehman, editors), Scribner, 2001.

"Fretwork" also appeared in *The Best American Poetry 2002* (Robert Creeley and David Lehman, editors), Scribner, 2002.

"Moving Target" also appeared in the Signature Series of the Catskills Poetry Workshop, Catskills Ltd. Edition, 2000.

"Spoken Part, for Countertenor Voice" appeared as a Dia Foundation Broadside, 2000.

"To the Tune of a Small, Repeatable, and Passing Kindness" also appeared in *Pushcart Prize XXVI: Best of the Small Presses* (Bill Henderson, editor), Pushcart Press, 2002.

The epigraph comes from Royce's *The World and the Individual*. All thanks to my friend and colleague Naomi Lebowitz, for leading me there.